THE DRAGONFLY:

AN INSPIRATION
of REMEMBRANCE

Helena C. Farrell

authorHOUSE®

AuthorHouse™
1663 Liberty Drive
Bloomington, IN 47403
www.authorhouse.com
Phone: 833-262-8899

Published by AuthorHouse   03/31/2023

ISBN: 979-8-8230-0520-3 (sc)
ISBN: 979-8-8230-0519-7 (e)

Print information available on the last page.

This book is printed on acid-free paper.

Death be Not Proud, 1609
~ John Donne, English Poet

Blessed are those who Mourn for
they will be comforted
~ Beatitudes

DEDICATION

This is dedicated to my late son, Michael Joseph Lota and those who have experienced a loss.

The dragonfly gave motion to the voiceless; my remembrance gives voice to his spiritual life *Dragonflies have flown the earth for 300 million years, dragonflies symbolize our ability to overcome times of hardship. They remind us to take time to reconnect with our own strength, courage and happiness. May your heart be lifted by dragonfly wings.*

PROLOGUE

The Prophet
A sadness came upon him and he thought.
How shall I go in peace and without sorrow?
Nay, not without a wound in the spirit . . .
How often have you sailed in my dreams . . .
And you alone, vast sea, sleepless mother,
Who alone are peace and freedom to the river and the stream,
Only another winding will this stream
make, only another murmur in this glad,
and then I shall come to you, a boundless drop to a boundless
ocean.
~ Kahlil Gibran

A GIFT OF JOY
Poem by Helena C. Farrell written to her young son Michael

Delicate as porcelain is his skin. Like a blue sea, clear and bright are his eyes. Sandy hair so light to touch, but oh, that cowlick so hard to brush. Sensitive, talkative, happy are his moods. Almost four and his friend Tom Thumb he will not lose. Now comfort and security claim his friend Tom. But not for long, I feel in my heart, for baseball and fishing his hands will soon tame. He fills my heart with a sweet dove's song. Take care, he is precious. I sense he can break. Dear God thank you for blessing me with this special gift, Michael. A son I adore and angels guide his soul.

~Your loving mother

CHAPTER ONE

His Grief he will not forget,
but it will not darken his heart.
~ J. R. R. Tolkien

Serenity, peace, solitude, and remembrance. Sitting solitary on a special memorial bench in a quiet, verdant, lush, forested area overlooking an oval- shaped, glistening pond, with a graceful sprouting fountain in the center. The pond and surrounding area is bathed in the afternoon light. I am flooded with memories. Magically, a beautiful rainbow arches over the glimmering, mirror-like water. A proud, stately, colorful mallard slowly glides by followed by his dutiful mate while a few languid ducks follow. Surely, they are feeling at home in this tiny piece of heaven. Nature is fascinating, complex, entrancing and healing. Since it is late spring, the sun is warming my stoic face. As I sit here pondering over the last challenging six years, my thoughts flutter to and fro. A mixture of laughter, anger, love, regret, joy, and immense grief infiltrates my scattering thoughts. I am startled hearing laughter, taking me out of my meditation. Looking up, I observe a young man with two little boys holding fishing poles in hands, walking toward me. The man calls out to the anxious boys, "Stop running, you'll trip and fall." The larger boy responds, "Don't worry dad; we're okay." "Stop by that tree. The fish are plentiful there:" the father calls out to his sons.

In front of me, a massive Weeping Willow tree, rooted solidly in the ground with mammoth, unyielding branches gracefully sweeps over the luminous pond welcoming inquisitive, excited

1

children to safely climb on its inviting sturdy limbs or to fish near it. The restless boys place their fishing poles down near this particular tree. With help from their father, the sons proceed to bait the hooks preparing to throw their fishing line into the pond. Their restless anticipation of catching a fish is palpable. The ducks quickly evacuate the area once they realize there will be no bread thrown by the children. *Catching a fish is their goal.* The father and his youthful sons take no notice of me sitting behind them on the bench facing the magical Weeping Willow tree. At first, I take exception to their intrusion. I selfishly feel this is my special place; a place to connect with the past; to remember the familiar laughter; to hold on to my glorious memories. The smaller of the boys begins to cry. He is unable to throw his line as far out into the pond as his older brother; the father quickly intervenes. "Christian," he explains: "You shouldn't get upset because Michael's line went out further; there are plenty of fish along the edge." Hearing the father call out the names, I instantly feel lightheaded. My mind reverts back to that unforgettable, unfathomable night when my life forever changed.

THE BENCH

Come sit beside me and take my hand. Lets
share our memories from year after year
While our lives have changed in so many ways.
It's your hand I will hold the rest of my days.
~ Christmas Bench ornament, Roman

CHAPTER TWO

(Six years back)

The Unfathomable

What we have once enjoyed deeply we can never lose.
All that we love deeply becomes a part of us.
~ Helen Keller

Sitting stoically in the front seat of my local-town patrol car, next to a seasoned middle-aged patrolman, I am experiencing an out-of-body, hallucinatory state. Under the solemn circumstances, the kind patrolman is respectfully quiet. Out-of-no-where a pesky butterfly, fly, or wasp keeps annoying the officer by fluttering in front of the black and white patrol car windshield. This little flying creature temporarily brought me back to reality. The frustrated police officer put on the windshield wipers to frighten it away. This determined little insect is persistent. It follows us to the end of our short, unfathomed destination.

It is only right that I further explain why I, an elderly woman in her seventies, is sitting in a patrol car at six a.m. on a cold November morning with a policeman and her stepson Joseph Farrell. The sun is slowly rising yet there is darkness surrounding my aching soul. Allow me to reflect back to that harrowing night when my life was permanently altered forever. It was a typical fall night sitting with my husband watching television. We went to bed around ten p.m. For some unknown reason,

I was restless, unsettled and could not sleep. Not wanting to disturb my husband, around three in the morning. I quietly got up from our bed and silently sneaked down the stairs to our den. Hoping to quiet my unsettledness, I put on the television. I was sitting there no more than half an hour when our doorbell startled me. Confused and concerned but not wanting to wake my husband, I crept down the stairs to our front door. I looked through the peephole and immediately became anxious seeing a man standing there in a dark suit holding a cap. This stranger asked if I was Helena Farrell and if so, he needed to speak with me. *It was a policeman.* Being a cautious woman, I did not open the door. I insisted he show me his identification. He complied flashing me his ID. After I reviewed it, I hesitated to allow him to enter but something told me I should so I nervously opened the door. The officer suggested we go upstairs where we could sit down. Like a stoned zombie, I barely made it upstairs with this somber policeman behind me. Instinctively I knew something terrible happened. My heart was pounding so fiercely I thought it would burst out of my heaving chest.

Once in the quiet living room, the officer gazed around noticing the numerous framed photos of our adult children and grandchildren. Standing stoically like a marble statue he introduced himself and firmly, yet respectively, suggested I sit down. Trembling, I complied. It startled me when he asked if I was the mother of Michael Lota. My entire body shook as I cried out, "Yes, why?" *Somehow, I already knew.* He compassionately informed me of my son's sudden passing from a heart attack. Later I was told, Michael passed while sleeping in his lounge chair watching television. *To this day, I can't imagine how dreadful it must have been for his wife.*

My screams woke my husband, Joe. When he came down from the bedroom, and saw the policeman, he was frightened and confused. Frantically, I screamed out, "My son Michael died." Shocked he came to me and held me while I shook crying hysterically.

Evidently, I blocked out what happened next while my husband had to take over. After the officer related the tragic events to Joe, he was so distraught he called his oldest daughter, Teresa. As difficult as it was, when I came back to reality, I forced myself to remain calm realizing this was necessary when I had to face Michael's wife and two young daughters, his beloved family. With quivering hands, I reached for my cell phone and called Michael's two brothers; my older son Christopher and my youngest son, Joseph. I was unable to reach Chris but fortunately Joseph answered my call. Since he lives close by, without explaining further, I insisted he come to our home immediately. When Joseph arrived, at first my confused son thought something happened to me or to my husband. Not thinking clearly, I regretfully blurted out in pain, "Your brother Michael died!" Hearing this, Joseph started to lose balance almost falling to his knees. Needless to say, I felt horrible I inflicted such pain to my unsuspecting, shocked son Joseph. Eventually, we gathered our strength.

After talking with the officer and knowing I had the policeman and my husband to console me, Joseph left to go be with Michael's bereaved family who lived five minutes away. Gathering all the strength I had in me, I got dressed. Word spread among the extended family. As a mother, mother-in-law, and grandmother, I realized I must be strong for my granddaughters and my son's distraught wife. The next few days were going to be unbearable but knowing we must face the grief with dignity, acceptance, and love became my mantra, my strength, and Michael's family's future destiny.

CHAPTER THREE

(Back to present day: Six years later)

Human loss means the loss of the stories the dead
once told, in their particular voices.
~ Chimamanda Ngozi

Sitting peacefully and serenely alone on the memorial bench, watching the two young brothers fishing by that magnificent weeping willow tree, near the sublimed Thoreau's Walden-like pond with their father guiding them and hearing the younger boy shout, "I got a fish!" shocked me back from memories of that fateful day of loss into stark reality. The father rushed over to assist the little guy who was trying desperately and unsuccessfully to unhook his meager catch. Seeing the boy excitedly jumping up and down brought a smile to my face. With a sour look on his face, the older brother stood there in dismay seeing his empty line. I immediately thought about my sons Chris and Michael when they went fishing together; Michael always caught the fish while Chris looked on in utter disappointment. *Joseph was not born yet.*

Still observing the patient father unhooking the fish, I noticed a fluttering creature hovering over the younger boy at the edge of the water. The older brother went to swat it away but the father reprimanded him ordering: "Leave it be son, that's a harmless dragonfly." "Oh my gosh!" I blurted out. Hearing me, the father turned and looked at me. It seems like only yesterday when my sons went fishing on this exact spot. I waved my hand alerting him that I was fine. *But I wasn't fine.* Tears clouded my eyes and gently rolled down my face. That innocent, graceful dragonfly brought back memories of that fateful morning when the policeman and I were in the patrol car driving to my son Michael's house on that dreadful November day years past when a dragonfly flew in front of the police car. *Watching the two young boys excitedly looking at the fluttering dragonfly,* I felt Michael's spiritual presence. *The dragonfly has become a hopeful symbol that Michael is forever with us in spirit.*

Dragonflies seem so fragile, so ethereal, so mystical, and so otherworldly. "With their light, transparent wings, their shiny, iridescent bodies and the agile grace of their movements, it's no wonder that many people throughout the ages have seen these beautiful insects as being close to the spirit world:" MillersGuide. Now, whenever I encounter one of these symbolic creatures, it gives me a sense of peace, comfort, and acceptance of what is and what cannot be changed.

Since Michael was such a strong, solid presence, a monumental human, and a force to be reckoned with I would have expected a more forceful, firmly rooted symbol to appear whenever I perceive Michael's presence. Something sturdy like a bear, a shark, a tiger, or a lion which is his Leo zodiac sign. Yet, it is not, it is this precious, delicate, whimsical, blue winged (the color of Michael's eyes) beautiful but oh so fragile miniature creature. Echoes of a line from the poem, *A Gift of Joy,* which I wrote shortly after his birth come rushing back at me, Be *careful, I sense he can break,* haunts me.

CHAPTER FOUR

Everything you love will probably be lost,
but in the end, love will return in another way.
~ Franz Kafka, *The Doll House*

As agonizing and painstaking as it is, acceptance that my son Michael is no longer physically here is essential in facing the endless, enduring, life-altering healing process. Recognizing that not only have I experienced this major loss, but so many others especially his wife and two young daughters, his brothers, their families as well as his in-laws and his close friends. You become more sensitive to others who have experienced a loss.

You never really recover from losing a loved one. Filling that huge, empty hole in one's damaged heart is on-going, excruciating and all consuming. How does one reach the point where ". . . *love will return in another way.*" It becomes an unthinkable, treacherous, and endless journey.

I learned one must acknowledge the loss and accept the pain in search of inner peace. After the mourning period, which never truly ends, I gave myself permission to remember the good times and to laugh at the silly and questionable things my son, the jokester Michael did. After a sudden, unexpected, premature death, the need to place the person on a pedestal becomes an artificial way to grieve and deal with a major loss. Michael was human, not perfect. He was giving and kind;

stubborn, funny, annoying, generous, demanding, and to me, lovable.

The obituary article in the local newspaper included factual details about his life: "Michael was born in Ridgewood, New Jersey and raised and lived in Glen Rock, New Jersey. He was an avid motorcycle enthusiast, fisherman and commercial diver. Michael loved his family and spending time with them at the beach, at home and in everyday life. He played the drums and loved music. Michael will always be remembered for his sense of humor, culinary skills and the ability to tell a good story. Most of all Michael will be remembered for being kind, a selfless friend, caring human being, father, husband, brother, uncle, and son who only wanted the best for all."

In providing a more detailed account I would begin with my son's love of animals especially his beloved Atlas, a black Chinese Shar-pei dog, and his kooky, devoted pet cockatoo Tweets. He relished fishing, snorkeling, skin diving, and music. At an early age, music became his passion and continued throughout his adult life. The drums with crashing cymbals were his instrument of choice.

He took his years of drum lessons seriously and during his teenage years formed a band with a group of friends. As U2, Bono stated: "Music is the balm for the ache inside," I believe Michael found peace, pride and comfort in music. He practiced in our house, and also at his friend Kenny's garage. His dream was to become a rock star.

When Michael was a teenager and the family took a trip to Italy, when it came time to bring a souvenir Michael wanted only one thing. **Bongo drums!** Now where are we going to find bongo drums in Italy? We could not convince Michael to wait until we returned home to the states. He was annoyingly persistent. After much inquiry, we located a store that sold musical instruments.

Michael got his bongo drums in Italy! Later in life, Michael shared his love for drums and cymbals with young Anthony who was his close friend Gina's son. He gifted Anthony with his cymbals which Gina said helped Anthony tremendously.

As Bono states in his book, *Surrender:* "It is sorrow not joy that binds people together." I firmly believe that Michael's music and band mates were a source of joy and pride and accomplishment. According to Bono, in the music world there is a saying: "A drummer is born not made." This statement truly describes Michael who was passionate about music and a *damn good drummer.*

Growing up Michael had a great sense of humor and was playfully mischievous, at times annoyingly so. He was fearless, compassionate, courageous and fascinatingly unique. Anything with wheels captivated and engaged him. At a young age bicycles were his obsession, during his early teens mopeds and motorbikes were his main interests. Eventually, as he got older, the fascination and passion for motorcycles took over. Not only was he a skilled rider but he became an expert motorcycle lay mechanic. He treated his beloved Harley Davidson with kid gloves. Wisely, he knew the dangers and thankfully he respected the road and drove with caution - *hopefully most of the time.* He treasured long rides in verdant, peaceful, wooded areas, around shimmering lakes, and natural habitats. Snaking through coiling roads released his tensions, worries and captured his heart and soul. Stopping along the way for some respite and possibly a Wild Turkey bourbon shot was also part of his adventures. Riding on highways, and steep hills thrilled him and gave him immense satisfaction. He was devoted to his family, enjoyed his friends, and was passionate about music and motorcycles. *Michael enjoyed life.*

Much to my chagrin, Michael liked tattoos, or body ink as they coin it today. It still gives me shivers when I recall the day when he walked into the house and said he got himself a special gift for his sixteenth birthday. When he pulled up his sleeve and proudly displayed a tattoo on his arm, my reaction was one of shock. Clearly he marched to the beat of his own drum and not a literal drum. I thought his ear piercing was extreme but this was going beyond. "Now tattoos," I harshly reprimanded. Michael casually responded, "No worries!" He further defended this by suggesting: "Mom, you like artwork." Proudly showing off his tattoo he proposed: "This is body artwork." Speechless, I thought, do I laugh or cry? How about both!

After Michael found the woman of his dreams, became a husband and a devoted father, he supported his family with various jobs and careers. Early on, he had his own landscape business; then the dream, or as I thought, a fantasy of his, "To live under the sea," became not only a pipe dream or flight of imagination but eventually a future career. His wife, Cindy, was his greatest supporter and encouraged him to pursue it. Michael became a professional hard-hat diver; working for the government and private companies, and businesses who required his expertise.

Michael's dream of being a professional hard-hat diver brought back memories of his favorite children's book, *We Will Live Under the Sea*, by F. and M. Phleger. He requested I read it to him every night during his childhood. A fond memory that still makes me chuckle happened one day when five-year-old Michael decided he was going to live under the sea. He donned my apron tying it around his neck backwards and placed a small bicycle helmet on his tow-haired head along with swimming fins on his tiny feet. All set to go, he boldly marched down our property to the stream that flowed behind our house. It was shallow so I watched him carefully while he lowered himself into the water and pretended to be a deep sea diver. Needless to say, I hurried down and retrieved this soaking little dreamer and harshly, while trying not to laugh, reprimanded him.

To add to Michael's aquatic antics, in our den, we had a large, elaborate aquarium in our family room with many rare and beautiful expensive fish floating in it. One day, after Michael's stream incident, I found him with a snorkel in his mouth and fins on his feet, attempting to climb into our aquarium. He got one hand in when I leaped and grabbed him saving the frantic fish from our over zealot, future deep sea diver. *Clearly Michael was ready to live under the sea at a very young age.* A quote from *You Will Live Under the Sea,* comes to mind: "Now you'll have water all around you. You, like the fish will live in the sea."

A few years after these incidents, we went to Jamaica for a family vacation. Michael was nine-years old at the time. The family-style resort we stayed at offered scuba diving lessons in their pool by trained authorized diving teachers. If an individual taking the lessons were to achieve proficiency, he or she would then be qualified to go with a professional on a rowboat and dive deep into the beautiful Caribbean Sea waters to observe the exotic fish and magnificent-rare corals. *Sounds great, doesn't it!* Under the impression that Michael was at the safe pool with the instructor taking scuba lessons, his brother Chris, his dad, and myself decided to take a walk along the beautiful green-blue water's edge. We were stunned and shocked when we looked out over the sea and saw one of the professional divers in a rowboat with a young boy who was waving and calling out to us. *Yes, it was Michael*! As Michael's favorite childhood book implied: *Back home on dry land! What tales you'll tell. You'll tell them how you lived down under the sea. Someday you're really going to do it.* Michael truly did!

My dare devil child cleverly convinced his instructor that he was older and qualified. Michael signed himself up to go out deep sea diving and shrewdly charged the fee to our room. On a bright note, Michael came up with magnificent coral that he brought home. Back then taking coral as souvenirs was not prohibited as it is today with laws protecting the coral reef ecosystem. Michael's aquatic antics were foreshadowing his eventual dream to be a professional hard-hat working diver. He actually fulfilled his dream to work under the sea. His professional diving career ended when he became a father, because he knew it was dangerous. Michael became a welder and worked on varied construction projects. He eventually became a respected, licensed steam pipe fitter which took him many, arduous years to become certified.

Playing the drums, fishing, scuba diving, and fixing things, especially working on his motorcycle, were Michael's hobbies. As young boy he played and creatively built with blocks and Lego's. Drumming, building and repairing items comforted him and gave Michael a sense of accomplishment and self worth. There were times when things didn't go right, he lost his temper. *He was human.* These happy, personal remembrances bring contentment. Some not so cheerful yet brought about tender-cleansing tears. *Smiling Through your Tears: Anticipating Grief, by* Harriet Hodgson, allowed me to view tears in a different light; a way of refining the unending ache: *Tears are cleansing and restorative; they water the thirsty dry heart and ease the grief.*

CHAPTER FIVE

*Grief is allowed to come out . . . it's
treated like a gentle companion.
It should never be shooed away."*
~ Chanel Miller, *The New York Times*
(February 21, 2021)

In the natural order of life, the parent is supposed to precede the child into eternal life. *Oh, the pain when it happens in reverse.* When one experiences a severe loss, you never entirely get over it you only go through it. You learn to adapt and desperately try to accept what is. During the early stages of the grieving process, one tends to only feel the loss and not to recall the person. It has taken me years to laugh and talk about Michael in a good light and also to reflect on the not-so-pleasant things.

The stages of grief vary for different people and we must respect and honor each person's way of dealing with a crushing, life shattering, personal loss. Major and minor losses should be acknowledged, respected, and deemed it as a way to assist in restoring an aching heart. Writing this memoir about my son Michael is my way of dealing with my loss but more importantly, of remembering and honoring him and his life; good and not so good. Understand, *time does not heal; it makes you cope and adjust.* Being around other people who have shared grief gives an extra, unique attachment. The saying: "love heals all" is worthy but it takes time, perhaps even a lifetime. After a major and especially a sudden unexpected loss, love is not what you are feeling; a river of tears becomes a part of your DNA. *Grief consumes you.* Grief is an emptiness, an anger, and creates immense guilt; warranted or not.

"The sun is most radiant when it is setting. Although it disappears from you, it never dies." Michael loved sunsets. In his personal poem *Freedom*, he glorifies them: "On my way home all I noticed was the dark, blue sky with the yellowish-red sunset that cuts right through which gives a perfect ending to a perfect day." *Perfect ending*? Did he have a premonition? Foreshadowing of eternal life elsewhere. Honoring his prophetic words, on Michael's memorial bench, which I mentioned earlier, it has a bronze plate. Engraved on a bronze plate on Michael's memorial bench are his prophetic words:

In loving memory of MICHAEL LOTA
"No Worries"
We feel your presence in the glorious sunsets.
Mom and Family

As I gaze up at the celestial, brilliant night sky, and wake up to a glorious-luminous sunrise these strengthen my resolve to live a life of love and joy through his memory. It assists me in dealing with his absence and to continue to live life to the fullest while always keeping him close to my heart.

CHAPTER SIX

One Joy Scatters a hundred Griefs.
~ Chinese Proverb

Clearly, after a major and agonizing loss the living person struggles to search for acceptance of life here on earth without that person. One goes through a broad spectrum of roller coaster emotions. The destructive and invasive *if only* and *the whys*, gnaw at the gaping hole in your traumatized heart. They vary from exploring all the, "What ifs?" or "If only?" and "Why him; why not me?" From a mother's perspective I pleaded, "He had a whole life ahead of him to live; a wife and children to care for; why did God do this?" To heal, one must not focus on the *what, whys and if only*; it is about acceptance of what is therefore allowing life to go on. To begin this restorative process takes time and for each person at different stages and in diverse ways.

For the healing process to commence one must feel and acknowledge these distorted, various emotions. One must try to release the anger and deep hurt. You may question: *Where, when and how to begin?* Keep in mind that grief is very personal. I cannot stress enough that not everyone deals with it in the same way. People respond in various manners. Some will find release in tears, talking about the deceased person, and about their feelings, emotions, loss and anguish. Many find comfort in supportive family, caring friends, spiritual guides; others may choose to go into a safe personal shell to protect themselves from feeling the loss and pain. One might assume that those that shield themselves live in denial. Not necessarily so, it is because they shield and protect themselves from the excruciating grief and unbearable loss of a loved one. Everyone copes differently and most often professional help is required.

A person who has suffered the loss of a loved one has dealt with the complicated feelings of being left behind. *Grief knocks you off your feet.* The bereaved individual often desires to be left alone. I on the other hand, I found myself needing to talk about my son, remembering him. Never wanting to forget him was my mission. Remembering Michael keeps him alive and strengthens my ability to accept the reality of the loss. *How did I accomplish this?* I offer this unqualified but caring advice, if you are spiritual, turn to your faith; read uplifting books. Recall or seek out supportive prose or poems or search out respectable videos that offer comfort and empowerment. Most importantly reach out to family, friends, clergy, and worthy highly respected professionals for support.

A close supportive family is most important during an unexpected death or any major loss. If you know a family member, friend or someone who has recently lost a loved one, I urge you to reach out to the isolated family member, friend or acquaintance. If they need comfort offer it to them or, if they request you to leave them be, suggest they consult an expert on grief.

In need of help, reach out to compassionate family, friends, religious and special grief support organizations. Such as *Good Grief,* which assists children who have lost parents. This respected organization also supports parents who have lost a spouse. Good Grief has been extremely supportive of Michael's wife and his daughters. It is crucial and considerate to keep in mind to value another's method of dealing with their grief. Do not judge but I strongly reiterate, if you fear they may harm themselves, insist and assist them in getting immediate help.

It is essential to recognize and respect all those who are also grieving and dealing with it in their own way. Continue to support those around you who are sharing your grief; *there is strength in numbers.* Sharing your pain, along with compassionately supporting others in their loss, will aid you in accepting your own loss.

CHAPTER SEVEN

Place me as a seal upon thy heart:
Love is stronger than death.
~ Psalm 127

This is a powerful Psalm for healing. *It is a prayer of comfort and strength for me and I hope for others who grieve.*

Holidays can be devastating and especially challenging after the death of a loved one. As difficult as it is, try, to continue with the traditions which you shared as a family or with dear friends and neighbors. My son suddenly passed away a week before Thanksgiving. After his death, I was not ready to celebrate but I encouraged my family to go ahead and give thanks for Michael's precious time with us. Coincidentally, my mother died the week before Thanksgiving years before my son. Both loved ones died on the same date, November twentieth-a date that I have come to dread. I find comfort in the belief that Michael is with his grandmother again.

Since Christmas was not far off when Michael passed away, his brothers delicately asked his family if they would like to continue with the tradition of decorating the outside of their home. All agreed, myself included. Michael's wife, his immediate family spent the day celebrating Michael's life by decorating his home in the way that he loved. Our intention was to bring a little joy into our grieving days especially for Michael's devoted wife and adoring young daughters. Some might feel this was inappropriate so soon after his death, but we sincerely believed it was what Michael would have wanted. *It was a day filled with bittersweet emotions.*

The delicate dragonfly became a symbol of Michael's spirit for me. My husband and I have a small artificial topiary tree where a lovely three-foot golden angel with a lute stands next to it; *remember, Michael loved music.* When this tree is lit tiny blinking white lights glow like glistening heavenly stars. I felt a great need to put small mementoes on it that remind me of Michael. The tree contains different sizes of jeweled or plain dragonflies. Other decorations include a blue motorcycle, a tiny drum, and items made by his youngest niece Madison. I light it in memory of Michael; it consoles me. Eerily, there were times it would light by itself. Was this a sign from my son? *I believe so.*

Relatives and friends, hearing of my spiritual association with dragonflies and their connection with Michael, began to gift me with various shape and sizes of delicate, beautiful looking dragonflies which I now have them gracefully displayed in various rooms in our home. Seeing them gives me immense pleasure especially when the dull ache of missing Michael overcomes and consumes me; feeling as if I am missing an appendage such as an arm or a leg.

There are times during a period of grief when a memorable event occurs. One such occurrence happened to me a few years after Michael's death. While having my hair done at a local salon a young woman was sitting next to me overheard my conversation with my hairdresser. My hairdresser asked me how I was doing after my son's passing, and I related the tale about the dragonfly and how it comforts me. The young woman excused herself and mentioned she also had sons and how devastating it must be to lose a child. The kind stranger then proceeded to take her necklace off and offered it to me as a gift. Much to my astonishment, it was a beautiful, delicate, silver dragonfly on a chain. Tears immediately rolled down my face. I emphatically said I could not accept it but she kindly, and strongly insisted. *For some reason I knew it was meant to happen.* This beautiful, generous soul quickly rose up and said she must leave to catch a flight back to Florida. She rushed out before I could properly thank her. Fortunately, I was able to obtain contact information from the salon manager and sent her a warm thank you note. Since that unique hap stance, we have become dear friends. This caring young woman lost a mother at a young age and now endearingly refers to me as *Mama*. Needless to say, I am thrilled and honored. We corresponded for years and met again in Florida. That remarkable reunion ensured we are family forever. *Signs from heaven come in varied and unique ways. It soothes the soul. Look for them! They are there for you.* My son shows himself under another form.

I once read on a greeting card: "Those of us who look for meaning in life's signs and symbols generally find it, then use it to help us on our way." The dragonfly and what it represents in relation to my deceased son does this for me. I view it as a symbol of Michael's soul. I am not sure if my son shared the same connection with the dragonfly as I do; however, he was an advocate for nature and animals and certainly would have supported my sentiment toward this graceful yet sturdy creature and the symbolism I've attached to it. This symbol and my belief that Michael is with me in spirit continue to bring me solace and guide me toward a path of healing and wholeness.

CHAPTER EIGHT

Everyone carries grief along,
his own burden, his own way.
~ Ann Morrow Lindberg

Even though most will find a true path of healing and wholeness, recovering from a loved one's death can be emotionally and physically traumatic. For a person who is trying to find joy in their life after an overwhelming loss, it is imperative that they seek out all means of renewing that sense that life is worth living and happy days are still attainable. Rising from despair and grief is a goal which can be and must be achieved to find solace in our hearts. We owe it to those who left us and to the living family and friends currently in our lives. Guilt and or self-inflicted blame will sneak up on you when you least expect it. A grieving person might feel it is inappropriate to experience happiness so they deny themselves any sort of enjoyment. The distinction between grief and grieving, even if it doesn't completely go away, doesn't mean that it won't change overtime. It is important to acknowledge that a more positive attitude will promote physical and psychological well-being.

Life altering changes stay with us forever, but it doesn't mean we can't find harmony in other ways, such as conversing or spending quality time with caring people. Also, in special ways such as praying, doing acts of kindness for others, any altruistic act is tremendously curative. Going places such as by soothing water, watching sunsets and sunrises or walking the beach all are therapeutic. Listening to comforting music, dancing around the room, reading inspirational articles and amusing-uplifting books. There is an interesting saying a *person reads not to feel lonely or sad.* Viewing beautiful art work can be tremendously uplifting. Physical activity such as walking, jogging, swimming, hiking are also ways to enhance your mood and make your body physically fit. A healthy body makes for a healthy, emotional and mental attitude.

The death of a child at any age is the worst loss with the most enduring pain. Though I put on a facade of being fine and enjoying the pleasures of life, the sadness remains. Anyone suffering this trauma must find ways to recover and go on living. The best therapy for me is conversing or spending quality time with caring people.

As heartbroken as I am, my deep love for my son gives me courage knowing even in death love remains and becomes permanent and stronger. Decorating Michael's home for Christmas barely a month after his sudden-shocking death, was his family's way of brightening our 'darkened hearts.' Encouraging us with the hope of enlightenment for the blessing of the continuing of: *It's A Wonderful Life.* This life-affirming favorite, classic Christmas movie sheds a bolt of illuminating optimism. The iconic Angel in *It's a Wonderful Life,* adds celestial, restorative contentment, and hopefulness.

I have worked hard to go beyond my anguish and to take pleasure once again in what remains. I am so grateful for my devoted husband, two fine sons, my six incredible granddaughters, lovely stepchildren, delightful step grandchildren and precious step great grand children realizing I can enjoy life while never forgetting my son Michael. As J.R.R. Tolkien stated in *The Lord of the Rings*: "His grief he will not forget, but it will not darken his heart." *Search and reach for the light to enlighten your heart.*

Memorializing Michael's life strengthens and encourages me that there is a wonderful life ahead.

In the bible, *Lament. 2, 18,* these profound and thought-provoking words move me deeply: "Day and night let thy tears flow in streams, give myself no rest, nor let they eyes cease to weep," giving me permission to feel the hurt; it also reminds me that tears wipe away and cleanse a distraught heart. Knowing that we must and will go on by celebrating times of remembrance is vital for the therapeutic process. This enhances the joy Michael blessed us with while he was here on earth.

One must learn to keep adjusting to change even while facing obstacles every day. Like the fragile dragonfly that flutters about unaware of the dangers that threaten it, a grieving person must do likewise and face the loss with continued life-affirming existence. One must learn to trust that life will go on; yes, changed, but with potency of living life again by gaining a sense of tranquility. It is essential for the sorrowful person to know the loved one, who shared this earth and life with them, will also be with them as a part of their life in spirit. Yes, perhaps in a special, different way but they will forever be a part of them. With this in mind we gain the ability to trust again, to believe again, to quote the late author Leo F. Buscaglia: "An investment in life is an investment in change . . . adjusting to change and the joy of living leads to a path toward completeness."

CHAPTER NINE

—————O

*We draw our strength from the very despair in which
we have been forced to live. We shall Endure.*
~ Cesar Chavez

As mentioned earlier, certain days and dates such as holidays, births, and death profoundly affect those who experience a great loss. Strange as it may seem, one would assume the day the loved one died would be the most difficult. *Not so for me.* It is the date my son Michael was born, August 4th, his birthday. Prior to Michael's death, much loss occurred in my life. The death of my dear parents, my precious older sister Annette and many adored aunts and uncles, fun cousins, devoted friends and others who have deeply impacted my life. The grief I experienced in the past with the death of loved ones did not shield or prepare me for the experience of my son's death and the incessant, recurring pain. Every year when Michael's birthday comes around, without even realizing it, I become extremely mournful and heartbroken. A deep yearning to hold him in my arms not only when he was a child, but also an immense longing to hug him even as a mature man became an obsession for me. Realizing this could not be, I found a way to make the yearning cease by yearly celebrating Michael's birthday.

After Michael passed, his birthday celebration became a relaxed-annual ritual with my other two sons, Christopher, my oldest and Joseph my youngest. You got it! *Michael was the middle child.* His brothers and I would go to the arboretum where the memorial bench honoring Michael is located. This special commemorative bench is behind the magnificent Weeping Willow tree and the magical pond where Michael and his brothers fished, ice skated and who knows what else active boys do when they are teenagers. I usually bring a festive but manly Happy Birthday balloon to release into the sky as we sing *Happy Birthday*. Michael did not like fanfare or celebrating his birthday, but we do it anyway even knowing he was looking down saying, "No birthday celebrations!"

Celebrating Michael's birthday has become a yearly ritual and a time to reminisce the funny things about Michael also some interesting antics our comedian son and brother did to make us laugh or make us angry. Afterwards, we go to the Glen Rock Inn, our town's local pub and restaurant to raise a toast to Michael with a shot of the bourbon whiskey *Wild Turkey* his favorite liquor. *That stuff can put hair on your chest.* Some of the locals who happen to be there, or other family members, come to share a *Wild Turkey* shot and toast with us. It is a celebratory, yearly occasion. This is a way to keep Michael in our lives and to acknowledge his heavenly life. *Hence his birthday is festive and joyful.* Much to his chagrin.

CHAPTER TEN

———————O

*Two Things in life greatly change you and you
are never the same: lost love and grief.*

I must warn you, even as years pass and life moves forward, out of the blue something might trigger or perhaps nothing but that bittersweet, agonizing loss will overwhelm you. This year it happened to me! As I discussed in the previous chapter, my sons and I meet at our town's beautiful arboretum to honor and celebrate Michael's birthday. I was very much looking forward to it this particular year. I had a colorful, fun birthday card and a large paper dragonfly to put on Michael's memorial bench. I left out the celebratory balloons since releasing them into the atmosphere is hazardous to the environment and animals. Since Michael respected and loved animals, as we do also, balloon releasing is no longer our ritual on Michael's birthday.

This is a cautionary tale. What I am about to tell you, do not feel you have lost permanent control, or that life will not get better. This year the arrangements, as customary, were made with my sons to meet at the arboretum on Michael's birthday. On the morning of Michael's birthday, I lost control of my emotions, and my grief was surprisingly overwhelming. For some unknown reason, at least I thought, since it was six years since his passing, I would be fine. *Not so!* I was beyond melancholy. That morning, I got up as usual, did my daily routine yet the heaviness I felt for the loss of my son became unbearable. Tears were cascading down my face uncontrollably. I was weepy, like the infamous Willow tree at the arboretum.

As if I were in a time capsule, flashbacks of the day Michael was born transported me back. I thought about the day before he was born. Michael's dad and his two uncles decided to go fishing that day. It was fine since I was not due for a week or so and I felt good. My sister Annette, her young daughter Geralyn and my sister-law Sandra, came by to keep me and my oldest son Chris, who was almost three, company. We had a lovely day eating, chatting, and keeping Chris and his two-year-old cousin Geralyn busy. When early evening came around and our husbands had not come home, I told my sister and sister-in-law they could leave reassuring them that I would be fine. They left. I put my sleepy son Chris to bed. Afterwards, I had an unusual amount of energy, so I began to frantically clean the house. When my husband came home, he was exhausted from being on a fishing boat all day in extreme heat so he wanted to simply take a shower and jump into bed and fall asleep. This was *not going to happen. I was in labor!* At first, he thought it was false labor but after talking to the doctor who insisted my husband bring me to the hospital immediately, he called my mother-in-law Jean to come stay with Chris.

A short time after we arrived at the hospital, I delivered a beautiful, blue-eyed, bouncing 6 lb. 6 oz baby boy. *Michael Joseph entered our lives.* Even though I thought a little girl would be nice, seeing his beautiful, round, porcelain face and head of blond hair the thought of a daughter immediately dissolved. Michael was a beacon of light, a marvelous addition to our family. A playmate for our son Christopher. These memories overwhelmed me with an immense loss after Michael's death.

The day we were going to celebrate his birthday all I thought about was the much-loved morning when Michael was born. Even though years have passed since his death, I was grieving and mourning as if it just happened. *This deceived me.* My raw emotions resurfaced after being locked away in my closed heart these few years. Like the *Loch Ness Monster Mystery* my deep sorrow reemerged causing me an immense ache. A deep longing for the past life when Michael was still with us consumed me. I cried the entire day! Missing him. I lit a candle in front of his photo and put the lights on his memorial artificial tree in our living room covered now with many striking dragonfly symbols.

Thankfully, Michael's oldest daughter stopped by that day. We had a pleasant visit. With her marvelous operatic voice, with deep passion, Michael's oldest daughter sang the *Ave Maria* for my husband and me. *I know Michael heard it too.* Later that day, as planned, I met my two sons at the arboretum where we did our annual, enjoyable birthday ritual. Still, like an endless waterfall, I couldn't seem to keep the tears from flowing. I held all this hidden from my sons since their loss is immense also. Desperately I tried to keep them from seeing me sad. I knew they were also feeling the grief but out of love, they hid it from me.

This intimate story is told to alert those who suffer a loss and to allow them to comprehend that grief lives forever in those who have experienced a loss. Do not feel guilty or ashamed after many years this black-eyed monster of grief reemerges. Give yourself permission to feel the pain knowing it is normal but keep in mind that happiness will always be in your life perhaps differently but there. While at the arboretum, two beautiful fluttering dragonflies came by at the edge of the pond across from the memorial bench right in front of me. Immediately this lightened my somber mood. I whispered to them and thanked them for letting me know that my son was watching over me and wanted me to be happy. *And yes, it did!*

CHAPTER ELEVEN

○———

Those We Love are Never Forgotten

Birth and death seem to go hand in hand. No one can avoid it. Like his birth, Michael's death was honored. A few days after his passing there was a beautiful Memorial service performed at The Church of the Good Shepherd in Glen Rock where Cindy, Michael and his two daughters attended. It was a respectful, spiritual, and a comforting service. A day or two prior to the service, Cindy, Michael's wife, organized a meeting at her home with the minister and immediate family. After the planning for Michael's service was completed, the minister asked if a family member would like to say a few personal words about Michael at the service. Understandably, no one felt they were emotionally able to do so. *Truly I was not in any shape to say yes.* I thought!

I went home that night and sat down and wrote something to say about Michael. Never dreaming I could or would read it. The next morning, as we sat in the church prior to the commencement of the memorial mass the endearing minister came up to the immediate family and once again asked if anyone would care to say a few words. No one responded. I kept what I wrote in my purse from the night before, but still not sure that I could read it. The minister was ready to go back to the altar and I somehow mustered up the courage to respond, "Yes, Reverend Spencer, I will say a few words." Hearing this, my sons and family looked at me shocked. My son Chris, leaned over and whispered: "Mom, you sure you can do this? I replied, "I must!" After beautiful hymns, religious sermons, and prayers, Dr. Spencer asked me to come up to the podium to say a few words. I slowly stood up, shaking I walked to the podium. My eyes never looked at the many people who came to show their respect to Michael and his family. Leaning on the podium, I placed the small piece of paper in front of me, inhaled deeply, paused a moment and miraculously the words flowed out:

> *I am proud to say that I am the mother of Michael Lota. You all knew him as a big, rugged, tattooed guy who loved to ride his Harley, and would stand up and protect his family and friends at any cost. He adored his wife, daughters, brothers, sister-in-law's, nieces, devoted in-laws, cousins, and his entire family and friends. He was genuine; what you saw is what you got with Mikey. He worked hard, played hard, and loved deeply. If you were fortunate to be a part of his life, you made a loyal friend forever. He was a loyalist; a huggable Teddy Bear; a Gentle Giant with a huge, lovable heart. I paused here for a moment thinking I couldn't go on, but I knew I had to. I continued: There is a softer, vulnerable side of my son that few saw or knew of Michael. When he was in his junior or senior year in Glen Rock High School, he wrote this poem. I looked up and asked, Michael, I hope you don't mind me sharing this and I continued to read his poem **Freedom**.*

I read the poem, looked up and said, "Son, you have your wings. Soar like an Eagle. You are Free now. We'll never forget you. Love forever, your mom." I left the podium with tears dripping down my face yet relieved and overjoyed I did it. My son Joseph whispered: "Mom, how did you do this?" I responded,

"I brought your brother Michael into this world, and I will take him out of it with dignity." *A mother's love is never ending.*

When the service was over and we were leaving the church, outside in the parking lot some of Michael's biker friends respectfully were outside standing next to their motorcycles; this was their way of honoring their dear Hog friend. My heart leaped for joy seeing them. Words were not necessary, their act of showing up with their shiny bikes said it all. Later, in front of the restaurant for the repast, I was surprised, touched, and pleased to see Michael's beloved, shiny-blue Harley parked there. My two sons and I joyfully and proudly had a photo taken next to it. Standing near it and holding one of the handlebars, I sensed the rumbling sound of the motor and could hear drums beating; for me it was Michael's heavenly heart and soul.

The heartache and shock of losing my son is still just unimaginable. I know now that strength and comfort is always there waiting to empower the bereaved. I cannot stress enough, finding comfort after a major and defining loss is not easy but can and will be accomplished. After time, those around you tend to forget what happened in your life. Not because they do not care, nor have compassion, but their own life's challenges invade their ability to continue to comfort you. Some believe and profess that grief should be left behind and not consume you. Grief for some is an unpleasant word which conjures up sadness, loneliness, and isolation. For those who experience grief differently, they caringly advocate: "Grief is an expression of love!" A positive thought. *I find that to be true.* For some they believe, and advocate grief should be hidden or suppressed. They feel it is unhealthy; they profess love and grief do not go together; however, I accept as true that grief expresses deep abiding love for the ones you lost. One should never feel ashamed or make excuses for expressing their sadness; it is an air of endearment for the cherished ones they never want to be forgotten. Through remembrance and love a spirited bond will never be broken. *Keeping your heavenly loved one alive in your heart is paramount and essential for healing.*

I do not advocate wallowing in grief and have it become detrimental to one's health, daily life, careers, vocations, or friendships. Finding the balance of sorrow, acceptance and love is necessary. I strongly believe even in death love remains, no shame in expressing it. *Love gives you valor.* I found this to be curative and true. Remembering and loving Michael keeps him alive for me in my heart. I know Michael would want all those left behind to have the strength, durability to survive and live life to the fullest. As inconceivable as it may sound, I believe in advocating might through loss. Loss can assist you in finding new life.

CHAPTER TWELVE

——————O

**The student gains by daily increment. The
Way is gained by daily loss.**
~Chaung Tzu

The way to happiness is gained by loss. It seems preposterous to suggest that loss is the route to happiness. Life is a journey, a unique roadmap with countless twists and turns. This is evident not only through personal losses but through historical documentation about devastating wars followed by joyful peaceful time; incurable and curable diseases; destructive and curative climate; death defying environmental disasters and major scientific accomplishments to alleviate these disasters. Our personal lives must also endure these elements; we learn to bear personal and physical losses and search for answers of acceptance to tolerate life's critical events with positivity. *Grief does not pick and choose time or place.* Curing and relieving the pain of loss can be slow and agonizing but with the right roadmap of life and acceptance it *will* be reached. One must desire to travel that difficult road of healing and acceptance with resilience and boldness. Queen Elizabeth I Quote: "Grief never ends ...But it changes. It's passage, not a place to stay. Grief is not a sign of weakness, nor a lack of Faith...It is the price of love."

A good practice, when the time is right, is to embrace our sorrow and try not to wallow in guilt; thus finding: "The road back to joy," according to John E. Welshons in his inspirational book, "Awakening from Grief." To reiterate, grief is an expression of love emphasizing that those we love are never forgotten. Navigating back to happiness can, must and will be found. *Even in death love remains.* In Mitch Albom's life-affirming, compassionate memoir, *Tuesdays with Morrie*, the author quotes his devoted, dying friend and former professor/mentor, Morrie, with these profound words: "Death ends life not a relationship." Profound and beautiful words about lasting, pure relationships even after death. How deeply these powerful, reassuring words moved me years back when I first read them. Especially now, recalling and rereading Morrie's profound words, I find solace, comfort, peace and unending love more so.

CHAPTER THIRTEEN

O

Music is the Universal Language of Mankind.
~ Henry Wadsworth Longfellow

There are various ways to keep your deceased loved one alive in your heart and to store their life as an indelible lasting memory. Along with the memorial bench, Michael's family collectively decided to create a *Michael J. Lota Memorial Music Scholarship Fund* at Glen Rock High School where he graduated from along with his wife Cindy, and later both his daughters, and in a few years nieces Sophia and Madison. As mentioned earlier, Michael loved all types of music along with his oldest daughter. She graduated from Ithaca College with a Music degree, sang at Carnegie Hall and at opera schools and varied musical respectable venues, statewide and internationally. *Hence, the music scholarship had great meaning.*

The scholarship fund established in Michael's name enables a promising music student to seek advanced training in this field. Since the music scholarship was established, each year a monetary award is given to a graduating student from Glen Rock High School who will pursue musical studies. The funds originally were supported by Michael's numerous and generous family, friends, and charitable people. After Michael's death was announced, the family requested, in lieu of flowers, a donation toward a scholarship fund in memory of Michael. The process requires that the identity of the student applicants is not revealed to the committee members. The winner is chosen for their music ability. The anonymous applicant is chosen by the music department faculty solely for their academic aptitude and keen interest in pursuing a career or education in the musical field. *The Lota family has no part in choosing the recipient.* I am pleased and thrilled to report that the scholarship continues to this day.

From the onset of the scholarship, Michael's wife and daughter have had the privilege of presenting the memorial award. I was given the privilege when they were not able to do so. When the day arrived for me to give the presentation in front of the entire graduating class, family, friends, staff, teachers, and honored guests needless to say, I was anxious and nervous. I prayed I would do my son, the graduates, and the award-winning recipient proud. Other scholarships are also given on this wonderful day. All presenters sit on the school's auditorium stage and wait for their name to be called with a brief introduction by the school's principal. When I heard my name called, I took a deep breath, carefully stood up, and attempted to relax and gain courage. Under my shallow breath, I whispered, "No worries, Michael, Mom's got this." *Not really but I willed myself to do this for my son and his family.* Standing there at the podium with shaking knees, looking out at the audience I reminisced when I sat there years back at Michael's graduating class awards' day. Taking deep breaths in and out this is the tribute I proudly presented:

> *Legend Bono of U2 fame claims:* "'Music can change the world because it can change people for the better.'" *He knew what he was talking about. The Michael J. Lota Music Scholarship was established on November 20, 2015 to honor the memory of my son who was a graduate here in 1986. Michael was a talented drummer with a passion for all types of music. This strong connection to music brought him joy, comfort, and great satisfaction. He spread those feelings and the message of music to his family and*

friends. Michael's dream was for everyone to have a song in their heart because he knew music has such a healing power. It is our joy to see this award given to a Glen Rock High School student who shares the same passion and love of music. We hope this talented recipient continues to grow through this art and spread the magic message therein, as did my son Michael. I am proud to present this year's award to Glen Rock High School senior_____.

When the audience applauded and the excited student came to receive the award, my heart was light and flitted like the fragile wings of a dragonfly. Happily, I handed the winner the award while the audience clapped with enthusiasm. *What a living tribute! I felt Michael's presence.* As in Shakespeare's Twelfth Night: *If music be the good of love, play on.*

CHAPTER FOURTEEN

___O

Sunsets from Heaven
~ Helena C. Farrell

I believe and advocate that it can be cathartic and consoling to write a letter or in a journal to the person whom you lost. A few days after Michael's sudden death, when my emotions were raw, and I was filled with longing and love lost, I decided to put my feelings on paper. I wrote a letter to my son Michael. Sharing it with you may assist you in knowing my son better and to reiterate that writing your feelings soon after can be and is very beneficial. I do not advocate for all but for those that might benefit. I affectionately once again share with you what I wrote:

To my wonderful, fun-loving, sweet, giving, kind, gentle unique, one-of-a kind son, Michael Joseph Lota. You left us too soon and I, your mother, will miss you more than you can ever imagine. God wanted you and I fear you were ready to go HOME to your Heavenly Father. You always filled my heart with so much pride and happiness - I KNOW how *you loved* me, and your family. Also, I know how much you cared for your wife, daughters, friends, neighbors, the underdog, your dog Atlas, Tweets your cockatoo, your brothers, Chris and Joseph and Doc your stepdad. I am sorry that your earthly body let you down - it was tired and disappointing you - yet you rose above it these few weeks; worked hard and kept going on - pleasing everyone.

As a young child you had close friends. Some cruel people at times taunted you. You handled it the best way you could never let anyone know how deeply you hurt - that is a MAN. I wish you would have felt worthy of help - unconditionally - I was so proud of you as an Altar/mass server at St. Catharine's our parish church, a great town team baseball catcher, giving your best at wrestling - your culinary ability and especially as a fantastic drummer, impressive hard-hat diver - your landscaping business and in the end a certified, steam pipe fitter and expert welder.

A man of many talents - Michael you proudly decorated your house so beautifully for Christmas and kept your property trimmed, neat and your garden filled with colorful flowers and varied tomatoes. Your fabulous barbeque and other parties were the talk of the town...you were generous of heart, soul, and love. "Uncle Mikey" to so many ... your motorcycle companions looked up to you; your tattoos were a testament of what you liked. You were a free spirit but a gentle soul. You wanted the best for your wife, daughters and your extended family. Fishing made you happy - you were patient with it, and precise. You fixed everything for everyone who asked you. Your stepbrother and close friend, Mike Farrell, called you a GENIUS at fixing things.

You helped your stepdad Doc and I with a SMILE many times even when you were hurting, tired, and your health was not the best. You tried to take care of yourself the best you could. Have no regrets dear son you lived your life the way you wanted. You did it your way! I hope you were HAPPY. It was astonishing, or not surprising that close to 1,300 people paid tribute to you in death by attending your services on one of the coldest nights in the year. Many literally waited patiently outside in frigid weather for a long time just to come in to honor you in death; an example as to how much they cared for you. I am confident that during your life you helped or made more than 1,300 feel good."

I also wrote this letter to Michael soon after his death: "Son, I miss you but have no fear, MOM will be OK if you are at peace. I know your beloved grandparents, Atlas, Aunt Annette, your brother-in-law Charlie Lohr, friend Eric, and others you knew here on earth and now above will wrap their arms around you - FREEDOM is what you longed for and now you will have it FOREVER...Please let me know you are OK-guide me here on earth along with your wife, daughters, your brothers, nieces, in-laws and friends. Michael send me a sign so I know you feel my love. RIP my blue-eyed, funny, free-spirited-WONDERFUL SON - You always took care of me and Doc; you did it from the heart - I hope I did well by you as your mother. Forgive me if I failed you in anyway. Until we meet again, be my Guiding Light - I will pray for you here on earth-my special, wonderful Son. I love you, miss you, and so proud of YOU. Love forever, your mom. "

Thank you for allowing me to share these letters with you. It took me years to have the courage to show it. It truly was and is healing for me. My main intent and purpose of adding these very personal letters and writing this book is to encourage those who have lost loved ones to put your feelings into words on paper. *Writing it down is extremely beneficial in so many ways.* It is cleansing and rewarding.

CHAPTER FIFTEEN

Since Dragonflies only live for a short time once they reach the adult phase, they symbolize the need to seize the moment and live in the present - because the time we have to do everything we want is really only vanishing short.
~ MillersGuide.com

As mentioned frequently, dragonflies are my symbol for my son Michael. When I read the above about dragonflies, a memory flutters into my mind immediately. Shortly before Michael's passing, while he was still very much active and alive, I called Michael to come and repair something for us. He came willingly and quickly. After he completed it and did so with patience and kindness, I had this immediate urge to write something. I titled it:

My Hero: JUNE 2, 2014

Today my son Michael Joseph Lota came to our aid by cable jumping Doc, my husband's car. Whenever we call him to do us a favor, he never declines! Heroes are not only military persons, war veterans, doctors who save lives, police and firemen who aid those in danger but also the ones who come whenever you need them. They put aside their own needs and wants to assist others. Heroes come in various genders, races, cultures, appearances, and abilities. Age does not matter; wealth doesn't matter; only selflessly giving of themselves and not looking to receive anything back is what they freely give. Their reward is seeing a scared, lonely, weak, or needy person feel safe, contented, wanted, and important. A true hero is unaware that he or she is a hero. The real hero does not wear a medal, carry a gun or sword, cannot fly like Superman, move mountains; but the compassionate-loving hero makes someone feel loved. True unsung heroes pick up mail, bring food, walk dogs, care for pets, take out garbage for a shut-in; plants flowers, mow the lawn, sing a song; tell a joke or give a hug to a depressed, anxious, helpless, or lonely soul. A true hero makes flowers bloom in their receiver's hearts; makes music to soothe their loneliness; fills their empty stomachs. Small gestures such as shoveling snow; going to the store; painting; repairing; or fixing a tire can be lifesaving for a helpless or lost being. The hero's assuring smile make the receiver feel loved, needed, and wanted. You don't have to be homebound; handicapped, widowed, elderly or poor to reap the rewards from true heroes. . . you can be happy, healthy, wealthy, and a competent person to the hero; what matters to them is to HELP another person here on earth. He or she gives unconditional comfort and pleasure to another needy human being. Everyday heroes don't seek praise; they don't want medals, or financial compensation. Their reward is a smile; appreciation, seeing a tear of joy on the face of their receiver and to lessen the burden no matter how insignificant or major; that's what a real-life hero freely offers. Humbly they proclaim: "Why this is nothing." To the grateful receiver it means the world! The whole purpose for the hero is to hopefully alleviate someone's burden, fears, illness, loneliness, or sorrow. This is their sole and main objective. **That's a Hero!** May the whole universe shine on these altruistic, humble, kind and giving heroes. **Thank you, Michael, my son, you are MY HERO!**

I wrote this on a whim quickly but sadly, I never gave it to my son nor told him about it. To my regret and sadness Michael died shortly after. After all these years, writing this memoir and including these letters is therapeutic for me. Also, I believe in my heart and feel that Michael knows about it. Please, I urge you, inform those you love, honor, respect, or appreciate while they are living how you feel about them. Forgive when necessary. If you are unable to verbalize your sentiments directly, write your feelings down and share them. After you do this, notice how it will wipe away some of the tears, anger, and will hopefully assist you on your journey of renewal and strength.

Whenever I see a dragonfly, who, like Red Cardinals, are recognized by many cultures as a symbol of renewal and transformation, I receive a sense of peace and contentment. It is appropriately written: *"Dragonflies only emerge as dragonflies as the final act, after which they quickly die, which reminds us of the fragility ephemeral nature of life but also of the need to make the most of our time here on Earth and to make every moment count."* A dragonfly symbol allows me to accept in my heart that my son is guiding me and his loved ones here on earth.

CHAPTER SIXTEEN

The Strongest Person in the World is a Grieving Mother
that wakes up and keeps going every day.
~ SAYINGSPOINT.COM

Life must and will go on! That saying has been told to me by many grieving families and friends including caring people who mean well. True and wise words but as mentioned frequently in this tribute, *easier said than done.* For me it was a necessity. I had a dear husband, two other wonderful sons, their remarkable caring wives, their precious daughters and especially, Michael's lovely wife and young daughters. At times I felt as if I was sleepwalking through life. I went through all the motions of living; even had happy spontaneous moments and felt in control but I felt like a robot.

Unfortunately, out of nowhere something would trigger my sadness and consume me with agonizing grief. Echoes of spirituality, the *Mater Dolorosa* come to mind; the sorrows of Mary, Jesus' beloved Mother, also known as Our Lady of Sorrow. This devotion recalls the Blessed Virgin Mary's spiritual martyrdom in virtue of her perfect union with the Passion of Christ, her beloved son. Catholics and other Christians believe this was Her role in salvation history and what merited Mary's place as a spiritual Mother of all Christians or people with different belief system who feels Her pain and admires Her fortitude. Mater Dolorosa is symbolized by a single sword, or seven swords piercing Mary's suffering heart yet one who accepts the pain and loss and loves mankind. As a grieving mother, I *appreciated the symbol of the swords piercing Mary's heart* and I pray for Her strength.

How did I, an earthly mother who was hurting so deeply, and has endured so much loss, manage to rise from that deep dark pit of sorrow and depression? *I thought about Michael!* I thought about the crazy, funny, silly, wonderful, daredevil, ridiculous things he did, said, or did not do. The varied and numerous remembrances made me laugh out loud, get angry, and, or honored his storied life with a new and enlightening perspective. These memories woke up the mourning life in me to brighter days. It gave me the strength and endurance to write this hoping it would relieve the sorrow and place it in an optimistic and affirmative light and keep Michael alive within me.

An example of Michael's saintly and devilish behavior came to light when I came across letters written to his family after he died. Here is one: "While I find it so difficult to say how I will always remember Mike; I still think it is important to say that he was one of the most refreshing people I knew. I can honestly say I have never heard anyone say a bad word about him. We were all lucky to have known him. Love, Regina"

Another wrote directly to Michael's daughters: "I knew your dad as a very friendly neighbor. I was trying to lift a very heavy drill press from the back of my car. Your dad walked across the street and helped me unload it. He then helped me get it into my house and down the basement. The other time that I got to spend with him was at our Purim party. He came dressed in a red wig. It was the costume mimicking the bank robber that attempted to the rob the bank in Glen Rock a few weeks back. It was so fun to see him walk in wearing that costume. I came to many of your family's backyard parties in the summer. It was always great food and music. I loved his taste in music. He was such a kind and good man. He'll always be with you. - Hugh." These are just a few of the endorsements of the kind of person Michael was.

A testament of Michael's unsolicited kindness, one day, my husband and I were in a local liquor store when an unknown young woman approaches me. She asked if I was Michael Lota's mother. I hesitated for a moment then responded, "Yes, I am." This woman told me that she was a neighbor of Michael and Cindy's. She went on to explain one day, after a huge snowstorm, Michael, whom she hardly knew, came by her house, and removed all the snow around her property. She added that he adamantly refused to take money for it, and he firmly commented: "No worries," with a huge smile on his face. She told me that Michael walked away pushing his snow blower toward another unexpected, helpless neighbor to remove the snow. She mentioned that she was a single mother and Michael was a huge help to her. The reason she stopped me at the store was she was there to purchase liquor to give to Michael in appreciation. She asked me if I could recommend something. Of course, I said not necessary, but she insisted. I mentioned Wild Turkey bourbon; she smiled and said she would prefer getting something a little better. She eventually bought Woodford Bourbon, which Michael saved for special occasions.

Michael had a fierce passion for cooking. When he and Cindy got married and owned their own home with an inviting backyard, they frequently had BBQ's which were the talk of the neighborhood, as mentioned in the letter the neighbor wrote to his daughters. I can still picture Michael standing by the smoking-hot barbeque sweating but happily flipping hamburgers, turning long juicy hotdogs, savory chicken pieces, thick steaks, and spicy sausages. As I am writing this, I can smell the food, hear the people laughing and talking, and Michael joking with his nieces Nathalie and Chris's daughters Morgan and Rachel. He loved to tease and play with the children as they ran around the yard enjoying the fun festivities. His close, long-time friends Tim, brothers Pete and Pat, band mate Reggie and dear friend Gina and her family were included. Michael was a kid at heart, so this type of event was his forte.

Not one who liked to get dressed up; Michael usually wore a Harley Davidson T-shirt, baggy shorts, and perhaps a funny apron someone gifted him with. Macaroni salad with tuna fish was usually on the menu, an old recipe from my mom, Michael's grandmother Theresa. It was one of her favorite recipes. There were usually thick slices of heirloom tomatoes which Michael grew in his vegetable garden. Cindy and his daughters contributed with their favorite snacks and sweet treats. To this day, when I run into people from his town, they often mention the great BBQ gatherings and plentiful food and drink Cindy and Michael so generously and happily hosted. Of course, there were alcoholic beverages along with varied sweet soda for the youngsters. Plenty of ice-cold beer, an array of mixed drinks, and, of course, *Wild Turkey bourbon*. Music playing in the background; trampoline for the kids, and other fun things. Michael was a kid- at- heart but we never saw him on a trampoline.

Making people feel good about themselves; joking with them; helping them in any capacity he was capable of, Michael was always available for them. He was not always in a good mood. He had his ups and downs and when he was down you knew it. Although, he never showed me that side of him. His wife Cindy handled him well. He desired her approval and support which she freely gave him.

Others knew you didn't cross him or show unkindness to the underdog or a helpless person. It hurt him deeply when others treated him unkindly but tried to hide it with his macho bravado. His mantra was: "No worries!" When Michael was under the weather, angry, or hurt, he would hop on his motorcycle, put his helmet on and ride alone on long winding roads in nature where he found solace. The wind in his face and the road ahead relieved him of his concerns and offered him a renewed sense of peace.

Michael's adored daughters gave him such pride. His oldest daughter's magnificent gift as mezzo soprano opera singer Michael treasured and humbly admired. I remember sitting next to him when she sang in a choir at Carnegie Hall, this big-bear-of-a-he-man tried to hide while he wiped away the tears flowing down his proud face. Like her father she finds joy in music. Their youngest daughter loved dancing as an adolescent. Michael and Cindy supported her interest. Michael went to all her recitals and assisted in setting up the stage or break it down for them. At one point, she decided to learn, or Michael decided for her, to take archery lessons. They went together for her lessons. He shared with me how he was impressed with how well she took to it and was doing great! How proud he must be knowing that she is now attending Wooster Polytechnic Institute majoring in Mechanical Engineering and is working toward graduating in four years with both her BS and master's degree. At an advanced level, she shares her father's interest discovering and making things work.

As a teacher, Cindy, his wife, assisted her daughters with their school lessons while Michael was there to support them in their personal out-of-class endeavors. Being a husband and father was something Michael always wanted and thankfully he had that wonderful opportunity. Sadly, and unfortunately too short lived but memorable and fulfilling. *Memories and love last a lifetime.* I believe and have learned that love is permanent and never ending; it is eternal. As the poet Auden adamantly professed: *Love each other or perish. Through pain we learn, through love we are reborn.*

CHAPTER SEVENTEEN

I acknowledge that this desolate moment
Is the most difficult to endure
But it is, after all, just one moment
Be brave, my heart there's a lifetime yet to live.
~ *Faiz Ahmad Faiz, Urdu poet*

As the saying goes: "Life goes on." To endure such a loss, one must recognize and be cognizant that it is imperative you go on with your life even without the loved one in your earthly environment. I applaud and admire Michael's wife as she continues being a responsible, devoted, and compassionate mother. As a single parent she stands out and her two lovely daughters testify to it. As the above quote states: "There's a lifetime yet to live." Michael's wife exemplifies this. I am certain it is not easy, but she takes her responsibility as a single mother and encourages and embraces her daughters to make life as normal and happy as possible. Cindy is a mother and woman to admire and was a supportive wife to Michael. Through our shared grief, Michael's family and I have developed a stronger bond. It is crucial in loss to hold on close to our earthly family and friends. Stressing: "Be brave my heart there is a life yet to live."

Writing this testimony of love and loss brings back memories of the day my son Michael, in his early twenties, came to me and requested I accompany him to purchase a ring. This startled me because Michael never was into jewelry unless it was a simple earring for his pierced ear. After questioning him, he coyly mentioned it was for an engagement ring. I was confused but very happy. It was surprising to me to hear the young woman he was anxious and excited about asking for her hand in marriage with a special engagement ring was living in Washington DC. After questioning Michael, I was thrilled to learn that he met her at a party in DC while assisting a friend who was relocating there. Ironically enough, the young woman was from the same town we lived in and where Michael was born.

After obtaining the ring and presenting it to Cindy, Michael was thrilled she said *Yes!* His future wife moved back to our/ her home town. Months later they had a lovely wedding. After a few years of marital bliss, they were blessed with two beautiful daughters. *Life was happily moving along.* Michael passionately adored musicians such BB King, Jimi Hendrix, and Ringo Starr. This young man, my independent son, who had aspirations of being a rock star was now a husband and father.

Now, with family responsibilities, Michael recognized he needed to have a more stable career. Thanks to the support of his wife and continuing education, Michael eventually became a hard-hat, deep sea diver, his childhood fantasy. Finally, he was living the life he dreamed of working under the sea.

One of my favorite memories came to mind when Michael told me about wanting to get engaged and married. It was when he, as a single man, commented on his beloved dog, Atlas, was "a chick magnet." Apparently women noticed whenever he took Atlas out for a walk. Michael adored animals especially strays. These memories bring joyful tears and much needed pleasant consolations. In search of finding happy memories, you will find that the sadness will no longer control your life. Recalling, sharing, and laughing at these unique or simple humorous happenings lifts one's soul up to joyful remembrances.

After a great or even a minor loss, it is imperative that you recall and embrace the good moments. For me, these memories of my son Michael keep him alive. In despair, each person finds comfort in different ways, cheerful remembrance is my special way. I decided to heed the wise and empowering words: *Take charge of your life*. Along with applying these wise words from 19th Century Danish philosopher, Soren Kierkegaard who urged: "Don't forget to love yourself."

CHAPTER EIGHTEEN

There is an Angel watching over you in good times,
trouble or stress
His wings are wrapped round about
Whispering you are loved and blessed.
~Author Unknown

These profound but haunting words are displayed in my bedroom.
Years back Michael and Cindy gifted me with this lovely framed,
stenciled-scripted, spiritual quote. After Michael passed, I felt a
strange and urgent need to reread it. I notice the saying referred
to angels as male, (*His wings*) for me this seemed strange since
I erroneously considered angels as females. This spiritual saying
about angels reads: "***His*** *wings are wrapped round you . . .*"
(I know you must be thinking, what about Saint Michael the
Archangel). When I noticed 'his' I immediately felt that my
son Michael represented that angel watching over me and his
family. I felt Michael's arms around me protecting me. *It was
extremely reassuring.* Along with the dragonfly, I find solace in
these comforting symbols.

Another illustration, in my bedroom, on my personal desk,
I have a daily, spiritual, flip calendar which includes insightful
and enlightening quotes by Marianne Williams. As mentioned
earlier, my son Michael and my mom died on November 20th.
The day after Michael's death, when I flipped over the calendar
to November 21st, the daily quote was: "Death shall be the last
enemy, said Jesus." It further stated: "What He meant was that

we would no longer perceive death as an enemy. The spirit does not die, but rather enters new channels of life." For me, these were, and are, reflective words that soothe an inconsolable heart and restore hope and allow acceptance and reconciliation to move from powerlessness to strength adding periods of delight.

Even though I miss Michael dreadfully, with purposeful modification of what is and eventual healing, it allows me, and it will you also, the essential permission and force to feel happy, laugh, and enjoy life here on earth again. I eventually found this contentment through my extraordinary, supportive family, faithful friends, and new enlightened acquaintances.

After a seismic, tidal wave and life altering event, survival is an overused and sullen choice of words but that is exactly what a grieving person must strive for. Thereby reaching wholeness and setting in motion the sense of pleasure. It is important and necessary to recognize and acknowledge that your loved one is forever with you in spirit with eternal love. Thereby making the hard shell of protection which surrounds your heart become more flexible allowing you to experience happiness guilt free. In time you will find consolation through family, friends, professional help and/or spiritual guidance. It will be a slow process with setbacks, but it will gradually and eventually come to pass. Be certain you will overcome this deep, dark hole of loss through searching for and finding new sources of happiness.

CHAPTER NINETEEN

May every Sunshine bring you Hope,
May every Sunset Bring you Peace
~ Helena C. Farrell

The American poet, Joan Walsh Anglud wrote: "No man dies unless he is forgotten." Anglud also professes: "The unveiling of one's soul is the reason for Existence." Reflecting on years back when the thought of writing this formulated while I sat on Michael's Memorial Bench watching the two young brothers and their father fishing near that infamous Weeping Willow tree, I experienced a moment of illumination to reread the memorial plaque on the bench. When I reread the last line about the glorious *sunsets of life* which was prompted by the poem *Freedom* my son Michael wrote while he was in high school, I experienced a warm and comforting sense of peace. Usually when I read it, it brings tears to my eyes and, like the innocent dragonflies that zip and swerve around the pond as it did on November 20th, when I was in the police care driving to Michael's house after learning of my son's sudden death, these once annoying miniature creatures now stimulate a huge smile across my previously somber face.

More, wise, and worthy words from Anglud: "The unveiling of one's soul is the reason for existence." This sentiment also came to mind while sitting on Michael's special bench. The warm, bright sun was radiating over the glistening pond while a magnificent rainbow spread across it. Adding reassurance and a sign from above that all can be well, will be well, and IS well. I will forever grieve my son's sudden and premature loss but now I view and feel it from an empowering, comforting, spiritual and loving approach. "Through pain we learn, through Love we are reborn," Anglud's inspirational words once again restores my weary, setting sun soul to a radiant and brilliant sunrise of renewal.

CHAPTER TWENTY

Being a Mother was my greatest work of Art
~ Helena C. Farrell

Leonardo Da Vinci's most valuable and iconic painting, *The Mona Lisa (1503),* needs no introduction. Many years back when I had the privilege of viewing the actual work of this small portrait of a woman who looked so sober to me, I must admit I was slightly disillusioned. Her demeanor and dubious smile made me feel sad. Before I knew the actual history of the painting, I thought this is a mother who is grieving. At that time, I had not known such grief but I experienced it looking at this great piece of artwork.

Along with Leonardo da Vinci's infamous piece of art, Michelangelo's legendary sculpture The Pieta (1498), of the bereaved Blessed Virgin Mary holding her beloved crucified son Jesus Christ in her loving and longing arms which moved me deeply. I have a small sculpture copy of the Pieta in my room which I bought years ago in Rome. Although I've had it for years, I noticed it only periodically. Now I look at it daily and appreciate the anguished look on Mother Mary's sculptured face. It is both one of an expression of pain but also one of a mother's deep abiding love. These great pieces of art profoundly touch me now more than when I saw them in their original form. Looking back now, I realize that famous or not, iconic or not, real or created by geniuses, a mother's love is ever lasting, eternal, and never ending.

EPILOGUE

A dear family friend sent me this moving passage from the inspirational book, *Fragile Interludes*, by John Francis shortly after my son Michael passed away. Allow me to share this pithy but powerful section which moved me deeply and made me ponder long and hard of its meaning:

Life is short, and the things that are truly beautiful are often too far apart: A summer day at the beach, a sunset in the fall, a walk through the forest...But perhaps the greatest beauty that life can offer are those moments of closeness with others. Times of sensitivity, of understanding and sharing all of the kinds and times, - degrees and shades of love. Moments of closeness-the fleeting-fragile interludes.

Along with peace, happiness, and unending love, my wish, hope, and prayer for you is to urge you to search for and to appreciate and value God and nature's daily gift of luminous sunrises and radiant, scarlet-crimson sunsets as you continue and persevere on your journey here on earth toward inner peace and ultimate contentment.

My intention of writing this tribute of remembrance was for *my* personal healing. In the long, arduous process, I have cried, mourned, reflected, laughed, joked, and experienced a remedial-renewed conversion. A period of benediction was needed allowing me to experience a rehabilitated state of mind and a much needed and welcomed psychological and physical cure. This miraculous transformation restored and enhanced my faith, my life, and my future.

Wishing all of you who have experienced grief or tragic loss in varied and countless ways a magical, enlightened, spiritual transformation turning grief to hope, gratification, and everlasting eternal love. May your hearts be lifted on high by symbolic dragonfly wings, your special angels, and the wonderful memories of those whom you loved who have gone from this earth but now gloriously shine down on you from above illuminating and enhancing your mutual love. **No Worries, Michael**, I will end this on a funny, cheerful note as I visualize you riding or speeding down the highway of heaven on your trusted Harley. Son, your mother is always looking up, as I salute you with a *Wild Turkey* shot and fondly recall your affectionate words from your enlightened poem:

Freedom
By Michael Lota

As I rode along all I could notice was the beautiful autumn mountain scenery and the chain of lakes that lay beside the road. They gave me a feeling of peace through their calm, crystal-like waters. On my way all I noticed was the dark, blue sky with the yellowish-red sunset that cuts right through which gave a perfect ending to a perfect day.

Son, thank you for sending me delicate, magical dragonflies to let me know you are fine along with numerous motorcycles that pass me by daily while I think of you, need you,
or just want to know you are OK. Ride on and on into your glorious sunset. . . *Thumbs up!*

NO WORRIES,
FORGET YOU MICHAEL...... NEVER!
LOVE YOU SON FOREVER
Your devoted mother and loving family

A dragonfly will bring lightness
into your day,
it will help bring you joy
as you travel along life's way.
A dragonfly reminds you to be strong
and courageous too,
keep a positive attitude in all that you do!
~Author Unknown

I am the resurrection and the life;
whoever believes in me, even if he dies, will live,
and everyone who lives and believes in me
will never die.
~ John 11:25-26

ACKNOWLEDGMENTS

Writing this personal and endearing memoir was a labor of love. It could not have been accomplished without the support and encouragement of many special people. First, I want to acknowledge my son Michael's devoted wife Cindy, his daughters, my sons Chris and Joseph Lota, extended family and friends who during difficult times lifted me up and gifted me with their support and love making this memoir a bittersweet but healing undertaking. Looking back at my son's childhood and adulthood gave me the courage and fortitude to share his story not only through my eyes but his family and friends.

The logistics of editing a book is crucial. My dear friend and expert on editing, Mary Ann Tesoroni, labored through reading this emotional memoir giving me wise and professional advice allowing my emotions and love to shine brighter on the page. My daughter-in-law, Jennifer took the time out of her busy life to assist me in properly placing my words correctly on the page for which I am greatly appreciative. The new technology became clearer by the professional help from Joshua Asante (Cyp). I thank him! I am grateful to Munirty Awolu (Lu) who was a willing and conscientious reader.

My dear late sister Annette Mancini was my first inspiration for writing. We started writing plays and stories as children; she fueled my love of writing. This memoir would not be a reality without the years of learning from my writing professors' especially the late Dr. Kay Fowler.

My faith in God and knowing my son Michael is in eternal

peace fills my heart with unending blessings and love. Mother Teresa professed: "Death is nothing else but going home to God, the bond of love will be unbroken for all eternity." Thank you all for your lasting friendships and blessings.

In memory of my beloved husband, Joseph T. Farrell, MD, who passed away shortly before this memoir went to the publisher. He lives in me forever.

ABOUT THE AUTHOR

Helena C. Farrell is a produced playwright, a member of the Dramatist Guild of America and the Italian American Writers Association. Farrell was one of the recipients of The Student Achievement Awards for Excellence in Feminist Scholarship for The New Jersey Project: Integrating the Scholarship on Gender and is an elected member of the International English Honor Society of Sigma Tau Delta. Farrell completed her doctorate studies in literature with a concentration in writing. She is the writer of the original produced Off-Broadway comedy, *Room for Rent*. Farrell also wrote, The Longest Goodbye: A Memoir published in 2009. She co-authored the book, *A Walk in Our Shoes*, in 2013 with Geralyn Mancini. In 2017, Farrell was invited by Grand Marshall and Chairman of Barnes and Noble - Leonard Reggio and honored to be one of the one hundred Italian American authors to be a participant in A Celebration of Italian American Authors in the annual New York City Columbus Day Parade. Her 2020 novel *No Trick or Treats* was short listed for The Book Excellence Award. She lives in Glen Rock, NJ.

Printed in the United States
by Baker & Taylor Publisher Services